IST GRADE DINOSAUR BOOK NAME THAT DINOSAUR

SPEEDY
PUBLISHING

Dinosaurs first appeared around 231.4 million years ago. They were the dominant terrestrial vertebrates for 135 million years.

Tyrannosaurus rex is often abbreviated to T-Rex. The Tyrannosaurus rex was one of the largest land predator dinosaurs.

The T-rex measured up to 43 feet long and weighed as much as 7.5 tons.

The Velociraptor was a fairly small dinosaur. It was around 6 feet long and weighed around 30 pounds.

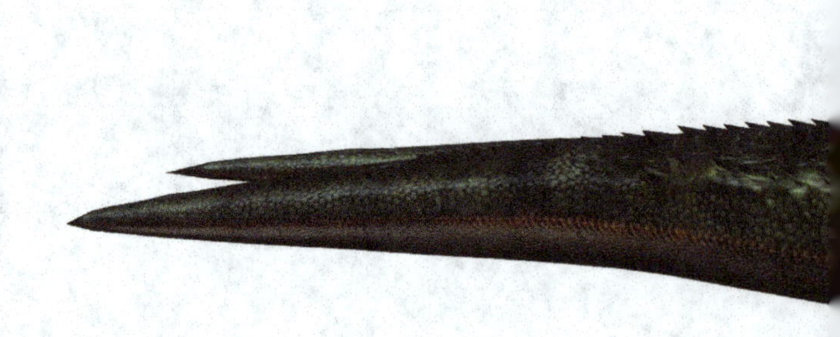

Velociraptor lived around 73 million years ago. The Velociraptor lived in a desert like environment.

Spinosaurus is best known for its tall, thin back spines. The Spinosaurus had powerful jaws with straight teeth.

Fossils of the Spinosaurus were first found in Egypt around 1910.

Triceratops means three-horned face. Triceratops was the largest of the horned dinosaurs.

It is believed that fully grown Triceratops were about 8m in length. The Triceratops was a herbivore.

The
Stegosaurus
is most
famous for
the diamond
shaped plates
that are lined
up and down
its back.

The
Stegosaurus
was large and
heavily built.
Stegosaurus
had brains the
size of ping
pong balls.

Diplodocus lived in an area that is now western North America at the end of the Jurassic Period.

Diplodocus had a 26 foot long neck and a 45 foot long, whip-like tail.

Apatosaurus lived in the Jurassic Period, around 150 million years ago. The Apatosaurus was a herbivore.

The Apatosaurus is one of the largest animals to ever live on earth.

The Allosaurus may have been the most fearsome meat-eating dinosaur of the Mesozoic Era.

Allosaurus had a large skull and walked on two legs. Allosaurus was up to 39 feet long, and weighed approximately 1.7 tons.

The Brachiosaurus had a long neck, a small head and a relatively short tail. These dinosaurs were herbivores.

The
Brachiosaurus
walked on all
four legs. The
brachiosaurus'
front legs are
longer than
its hind legs.